Riddle Roundup

A WILD BUNCH TO BEEF UP YOUR WORD POWER!

by Giulio Maestro

CLARION BOOKS

NEW YORK

A special thanks to Marco Maestro for the riddles on pages 18 and 26.

Clarion Books
a Houghton Mifflin Company imprint
215 Park Avenue South, New York, NY 10003
Text and art copyright © 1989 by Giulio Maestro

For information about permission to reproduce

selections from this book, write to Permissions,

Houghton Mifflin Company, 215 Park Avenue South, New York, NY 10003.

Printed in the USA

Library of Congress Cataloging-in-Publication Data
Maestro, Giulio.
    Riddle roundup.

    Summary: A collection of sixty-two riddles based
on different kinds of word plays such as puns,
homonyms, and homographs.
    1. Riddles, Juvenile. [1. Riddles.   2. Word
games] I. Title.
PN6371.5.M292   1989 818'.5402 86-33403
ISBN 0-89919-508-3   PA ISBN 0-89919-537-7

RNF BP PA CRS 10 9 8 7 6 5 4 3

What's a cookie with bite?

A ginger snap.

What's a measuring stick for a monarch?

A ruler for a ruler.

Why did the hen send her son to the store?

She wanted to pay by chick.

What's a hike up a scorching sand dune?

A hard climb in a hot clime.

When did all the bases get stolen?

When the team took the field.

What do knives and spoons dance?

Fork dances.

How does glue run?

At a slow paste.

Why did the grandma sheep put on a yellow dress?

She wanted to be a baanana.

What's a woodwind player's dessert?

Flutecake.

Why did the scarecrow cover his ears?

The caws were the cause.

What hang around together once a year?

Christmas ornaments.

Why did the pie shell go to the dentist?

To have his cavity filled.

What's a glance at a male goose?

A gander at a gander.

Why was the palm tree popular?

It had plenty of dates.

What's a fruity dessert for a shoemaker?

A cobbler for a cobbler.

When is a storm cloud not fully dressed?

When it's only in its thunderwear.

What happened when the pink flower grew?

The rose rose rose.

Why did the detective like his luggage?

They were open and shut cases.

What do snakes study in school?

Hisstory.

What's a ghost's guess?

Dead reckoning.

When is a fire like a lion?

When it's roaring.

What do you call fear of tight chimneys?

Santa Claustrophobia.

What do you use to brush a locomotive's teeth?

Tootpaste.

What's a wolf's favorite holiday?

Howloween.

What's a famous melody?

Noted notes.

What color did the cat paint his house?

Purrple.

What's a heavenly dessert?

Angel food cake.

Why did the runner put a net over her head?

She wanted to catch her breath.

What woke up the rooster?

His alarm cluck.

Why was the doghouse sad?

It was missing its woof.

What's a hot drink for a king and a queen?

Royal tea for royalty.

What do you call schoolchildren hiking up a hill?

A grade climbing a grade.

When is a daddy insect like a baseball?

When he's a pop fly.

What do you call a swordfight duet?

A dual duel.

What kind of pie is happy?

Cheery pie.

What are crowded caves?

Dense dens.

Where does a shoe make a phone call?

In a telephone boot.

What's a fitting outfit?

A suitable suit.

Why were the forks in a good mood?

They had many happy tines together.

What's a phony duck?

A quacker who's a quack.

What's a train car full of frogs?

A hopper of hoppers.

What was fishy about the singer's sandwich?

It was tune salad.

Where does Santa Claus swim?

In the North Pool.

What's a male turkey who loves to eat?

A gobbler who's a gobbler.

Why did the lion jump on his food?

It was lunge time.

What happens when a fire has too much wood?

It gets hearthburn.

What do firefighters wear on their feet?

Fire hose.

Why didn't the ghost stay locked in his room?

He was just passing through.

What does a bunny eat for dessert?

An Easter sundae.

What does noisy hair sound like?

Bangs.

Why did the bird put a desk in her tree?

She was opening a branch office.

What's a young lady insect in distress?

A damselfly.

Why did the captain quickly set out to sea?

He got an urgent foam call.

What is a strudel stranded in the sand?

A dessert deserted in the desert.

When is a book like a beagle?

When it's dog-eared.

What makes pointed remarks?

A sharp tongue.

What did the fish get in the mail?

A post cod.

What's a tall pile of cats?

A meowntain.

Why was the pie for the birds?

It was much too tweet.

What's a wet person?

A humid being.

When does lettuce become salad?

As soon as it gets dressed.

What's a vehicle filled with water?

A car pool.